LANG LANG PIANO ACADEMY

THE LANG LANG PIANO METHOD

MW01077223

LEVEL 1

Have fun becoming a superhero pianist with Lang Lang!

This book belongs to:

_____

My teacher's name is:

_____

FABER *ff* MUSIC

CONTENTS

© 2016 by Faber Music Ltd and Lang Lang
All rights administered by Faber Music Ltd
This edition first published in 2016
Bloomsbury House 74–77 Great Russell Street London WC1B 3DA
Music processed by Musicset2000
Illustrations by Lauren Appleby and Thinkstock
Page design by Susan Clarke
Audio demonstrations by Christopher Hussey
Concert pieces performed by Lang Lang at the Royal College of Music
Printed in England by Caligraving Ltd
All rights reserved

Lang Lang: worldwide management – Jean-Jacques Cesbron
CAMI Music, New York (www.camimusic.com)
Lang Lang: UK/Ireland management – Steve Abbott,
Rainbow City Broadcasting Ltd (www.rainbowcity.co)

ISBN10: 0-571-53911-4
EAN13: 978-0-571-53911-6

LANG LANG
INTERNATIONAL
MUSIC FOUNDATION

Hi, I'm Lang Lang! Welcome to the wonderful world of the piano. Learn to be a superhero pianist like me!

You can hear all the pieces on the online audio* and you can hear me play the concert piece in each section. The audio gives two bars of count-in clicks for each piece.

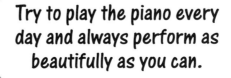 means there is a teacher's accompaniment available to download*.

Try to play the piano every day and always perform as beautifully as you can.

* Scan the QR code or go to:
www.fabermusic.com/LangLangPianoMethodDownloads

LEARN ABOUT YOUR PIANIST'S HANDS

LEFT HAND

Draw around your hand in the space given. Number the thumb 1 and the fingers 2, 3, 4 and 5. Finger numbers are given above or below the notes to help you.

Take fingers 2, 3 and 4 of the left hand for a walk along the keyboard on the black keys. Start in the middle and walk down to the lower notes.

How low do the keys sound on this side?

4
3
2
5
1

RIGHT HAND

Draw around your hand in the space given.
Number the thumb 1 and the fingers 2, 3, 4 and 5.

Take fingers 2, 3 and 4 of the right hand for a walk along the keyboard over the black keys. Start in the middle and walk towards the higher notes.

How high do the keys sound on this side?

GETTING TO KNOW THE KEYBOARD

The piano keyboard has patterns of black and white keys. The black keys are in groups of two and three.

Here is middle C – it's an important note on the piano because it will help you to find the other notes. Can you mark the other notes that are C on this keyboard?

* Check that your chair or piano stool is a comfortable height

* Make sure you sit up well with good posture

* Play with curved fingers, as if you have an egg or orange in the palm of your hand

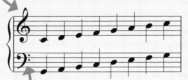

Here are all the note names on the keyboard: A B C D E F G. These letters are the musical alphabet and are repeated all the way along the keyboard. Can you fill in the other note names here?

Music is written on a stave – five lines with spaces in between.

Musical notes are written on the lines or in the spaces.

This is a **treble clef** – it shows the higher notes played by the right hand.

This is a **bass clef** – it shows the lower notes played by the left hand.

PLAYING WITH THE RIGHT HAND

♩ This is a **quarter note (crotchet)** and is 1 count.

Right-hand notes C D E

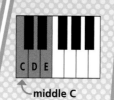

middle C D E

Let's get playing! Musical notes are written differently to show different numbers of counts. On this page they are all 1 count (beat).

Track ① **MY THREE-NOTE WARM-UP**

Jump to the next C up the keyboard.

This means repeat the piece.

Track ② **BOOGIE SURPRISE**

Track ③ **THREE-NOTE WALTZ**

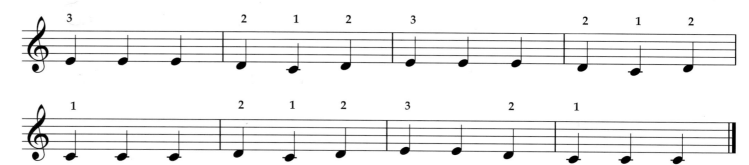

middle C

F   G

> Let's add two more notes, so we're using all your right-hand fingers!

Track
④ **RIGHT-HAND HIGH FIVE**

Track
⑤ **ODE TO JOY**

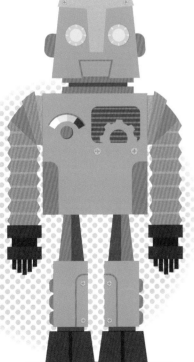

Track
⑥ **FIVE-FINGER ROBOTS**

CONCERT PIECE

Play the next C up the keyboard.

9

NOW FOR THE LEFT HAND

This is a **half note** (**minim**). Hold it for 2 counts.

Left-hand notes
E F G

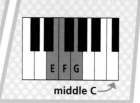
middle C

E F G

Great work! But there's something missing – your left hand ...

Track ⑦ **THREE-NOTE WARM UP**

Track ⑧ **THREE GECKOS**

CHALLENGE
How fast can the geckos run?

Track ⑨ **THREE GRASSHOPPERS**

CHALLENGE
How lightly can the grasshoppers jump?

Track ⑩ **SUPERHERO WALTZ**

Let's use all the left-hand fingers ...

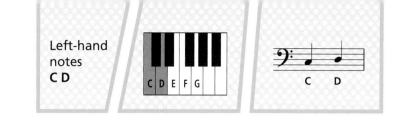

Track 11 **LEFT-HAND HIGH FIVE**

Track 12 **ODE TO JOY**

CONCERT PIECE

Track 13 **CATCH ME IF YOU CAN!**

The accompaniment starts here and keeps trying to catch up. This is called a 'round'.

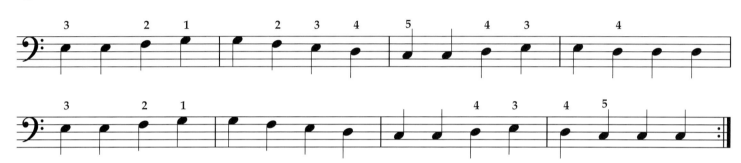

Find a lower G and C.

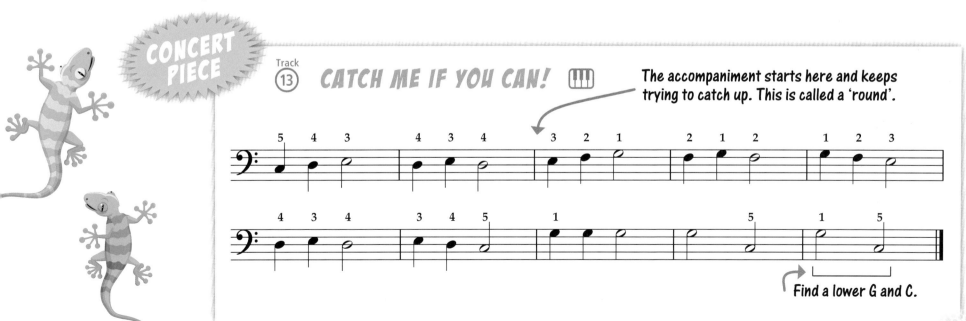

11

LET'S GET FIT

In music, notes are grouped into **measures** (bars) by **barlines**.

This is a **quarter-note** (**crotchet**) **rest** – stop playing for one count.

To be a superhero pianist you need to play lots to get fit!

Track **14** **LEFT-HAND JOGGING**

measure (bar)

barline

Track **15** **TOUCH YOUR TOES**

The distance between notes is called the **interval**.

Track **16** **SKIPPING**

Track **17** **RUNNING A MARATHON**

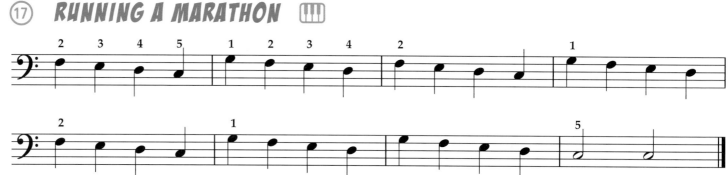

Now let's get your right hand fit ...

An **octave** is an interval of 8 notes, taking you to the next note with the same name.

8va⌐ = play notes an octave higher.

Track 18 **RIGHT-HAND JOGGING**

Track 19 **PRESS-UPS**

Track 20 **TURNING CARTWHEELS**

play an octave higher

Track 21 **GYM DISPLAY**

CONCERT PIECE

TIME FOR A BREAK

I love to look at fine art and listen to lots of different music to get inspiration when I play the piano.

Here's a beautiful painting called *The Caravan* by Decamps. On track ㉒ I'll play you *Of Foreign Lands and Peoples* by Robert Schumann to listen to while you look at it. How do you think the music reflects the painting?

Mary Evans / Iberfoto

LANG LANG'S THEORY NOTEBOOK

Trace over the clefs, then try writing your own:

start here

Name these notes:

Write these notes as either ♩ or ♪

E   F   C   G   C   C   G   D   E   C

Now play your tunes!

VISITING SOME NEW NOTES

Flying around the keyboard is important for a superhero pianist. Can you find these five new notes?

Track 23 **G POSITION WARM-UP**

Track 24 **WAKE UP, LET'S GO!**

Track 25 **HIGH IN THE SKY**

Track 26 **COMING IN TO LAND**

Here are the same notes in the left hand. The C is an octave below middle C.

Left-hand notes **G A B C D**

Track (27) **G POSITION WARM-UP**

Track (28) **THIS SUITCASE IS SO HEAVY!**

Slow down

Track (29) **PLODDING ALONG**

Track (30) **FLOATING ALONG**

CONCERT PIECE

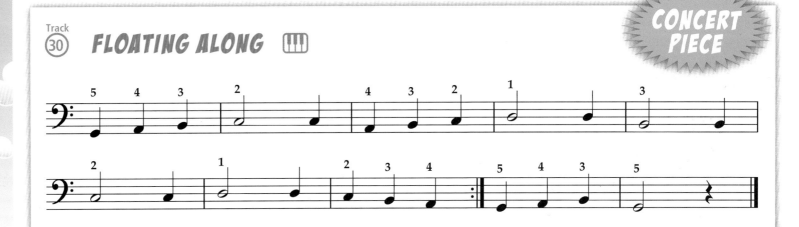

17

A TRIP TO CHINA

Count 4 beats for this **whole (semibreve) rest**: ▬

It also means a whole measure (bar) rest.

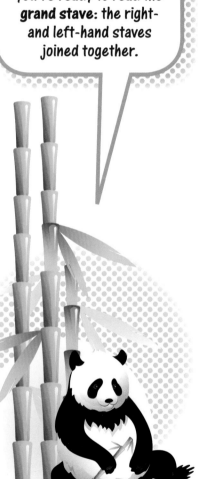

Let's take a trip to China! There's so much I want to show you ...

Your superhero status has been upgraded so you're ready to read the **grand stave**: the right- and left-hand staves joined together.

Track **31**   PANDAS MUNCHING

CHALLENGE
Hands together!

Track **32**   DISTANT MOUNTAINS

How quietly can you play the echoes?

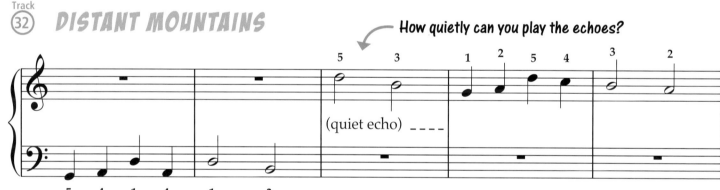

(quiet echo) ----

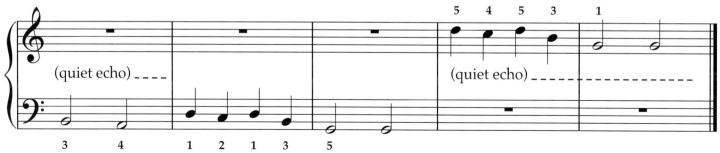

(quiet echo) ----

(quiet echo) ----

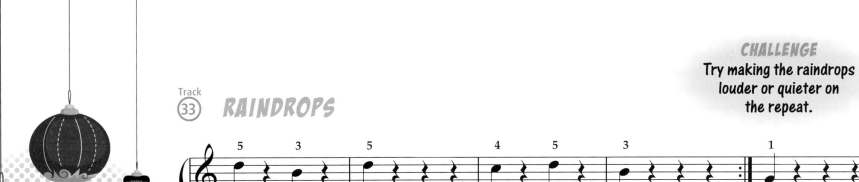

CHALLENGE
Try making the raindrops louder or quieter on the repeat.

Track
(33) **RAINDROPS**

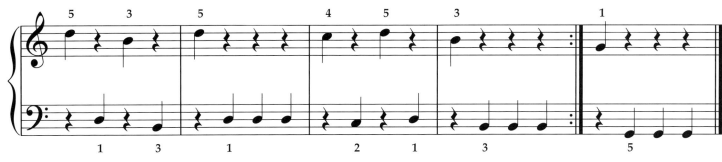

Track
(34) **LANTERNS GLOWING IN THE DARK**

CONCERT PIECE

A CHINESE FESTIVAL

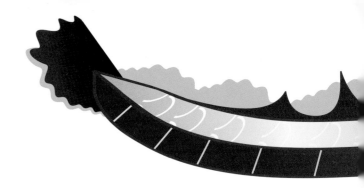

A **time signature** tells you how many beats or counts there are in a measure (bar). The top number tells you the number of beats and the bottom number tells you the value of the beats.

Track 35 ## DRAGONS ON PARADE

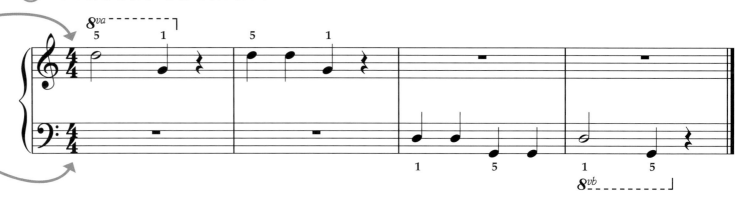

Count 2 beats for this **half (minim) rest:** ▬

Can you spot any here?

8vb----⌐ = play an octave lower.

Track 36 ## FESTIVAL FOUNTAIN

20

RED ENVELOPES

DRAGON DANCE

Look out! The hand position is different in this piece.

CONCERT PIECE

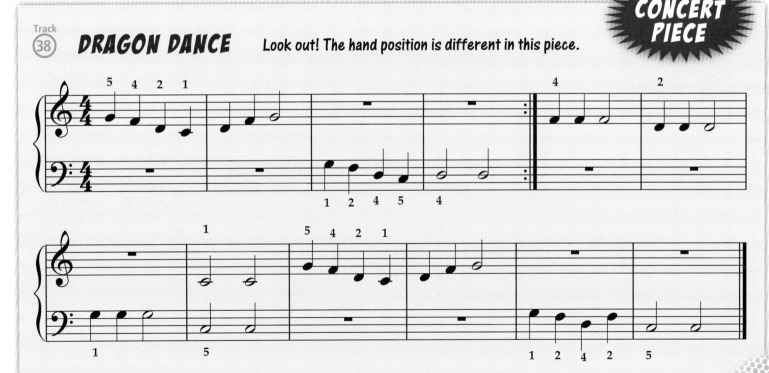

TIME FOR A BREAK

I love to look at fine art and listen to lots of different music to get inspiration when I play the piano.

Here's a famous painting called *The Gleaners* by Jean-Francois Millet. On track ㊴ I'll play you *Old French Song* by Pyotr Ilyich Tchaikovsky to listen to while you look at it. Can you imagine the women humming this tune while they work?

LANG LANG'S THEORY GAMES

MOUNTAIN RANGES

Write the note names underneath, then play the tune.

Write the note names underneath, then play the tune.

Draw a treble clef and write your own mountain range.

Draw a bass clef and a ⁴⁄₄ time signature, then add barlines and name the notes.

VISITING SPACE

Left-hand notes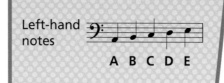
A B C D E

Right-hand notes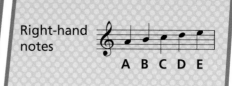
A B C D E

A B C D E

We're on the move again – can you find these notes in a new hand position? Let's explore them in space ...

Track **40**

5, 4, 3, 2, 1, BLAST OFF!

Can you go higher and higher, playing the note A all the way up the keyboard?

Track **41**

WEIGHTLESSNESS

very slowly and quietly

Track **42**

WATCHING THE RADAR

(All fingers)

like the beeps on a radar   *getting louder*   *'splat!'*

24

Track
43

A PERFECT LANDING

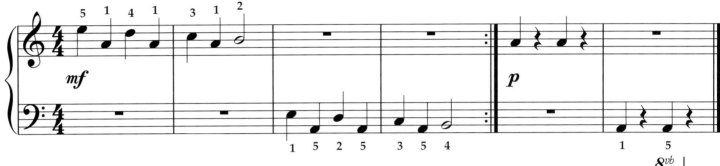

Track
44

TAKE ME TO YOUR LEADER

CONCERT PIECE

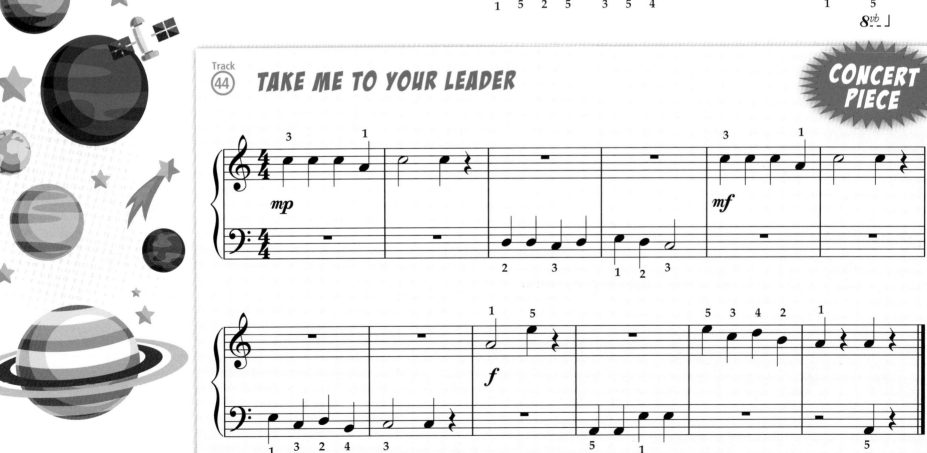

A SPOOKY WORLD

Ready for some spooky piano playing? I'm going to give you a new superpower to help you – playing chords! This means playing more than one note at the same time in one hand.

Track 45 — **ECHOING FOOTSTEPS**   This piece has 3 beats in a measure (bar).

Track 46 — **THAT'S NOT MY SHADOW!**

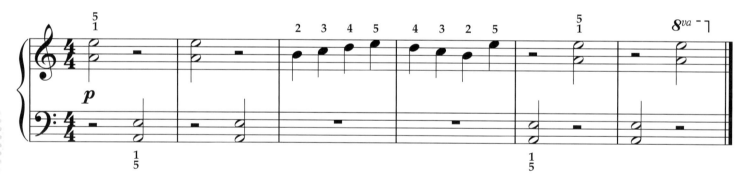

Track 47 — **SPINNING A WEB**

...in a tangle!

Track 48

THE MYSTERIOUS GHOST

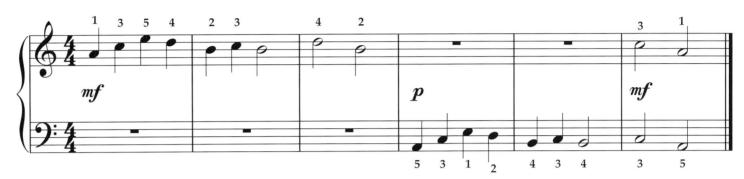

Track 49

HALLOWEEN DANCE

CONCERT PIECE

LET'S CELEBRATE – NEARLY THERE!

You're doing really well – let's celebrate! I can give you more superpowers as well: playing staccato and legato. Remember to check your hand position for each piece.

Track 50 **A SPECIAL TREAT**

shaking on the sprinkles

spreading on the jam

slowly open wide   *munch!*

Track 51 **FIZZY DRINK**

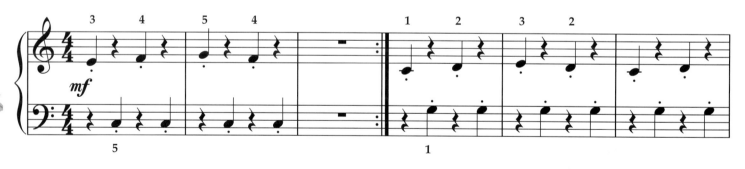

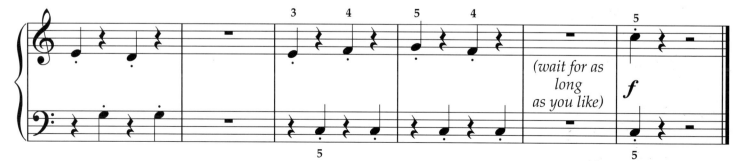

(wait for as long as you like)

28

Watch out! Check the hand position of each piece before you begin.

Track **52** **BLOWING UP BALLOONS**   Play quietly and smoothly until ... pop!

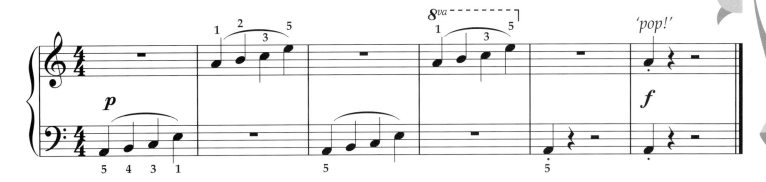

Track **53** **LET'S CELEBRATE!**

CONCERT PIECE

Play the right hand one octave higher on the repeat

PUTTING ON A CONCERT

Let's get your superpowers warmed up, ready for your final concert piece.

Track 54 **STUDY IN C**

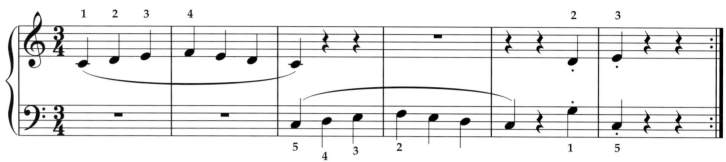

Track 55 **STUDY IN G**

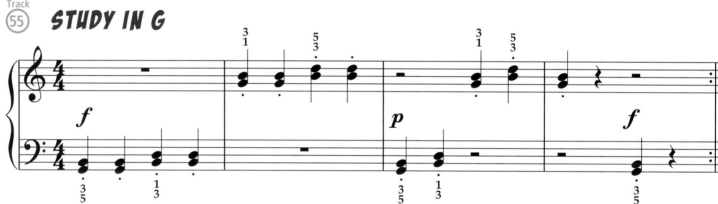

Track 56 **STUDY IN A MINOR**

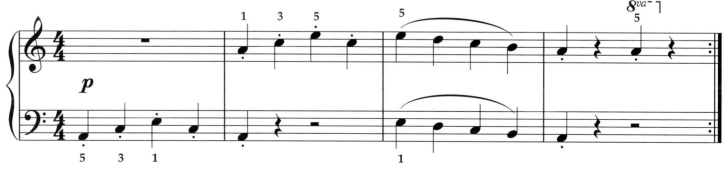

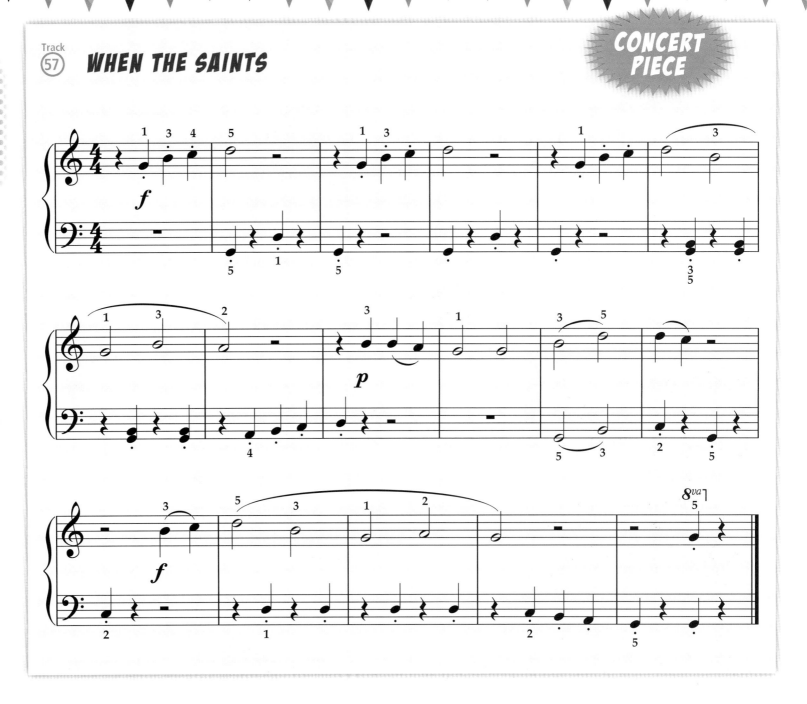

CONGRATULATIONS!

You've finished Level 1 and are ready to move up to Level 2!

Remember, it's great to do lots of listening. Here are some of my albums ...

Download a certificate for your teacher to sign.*

* Scan the QR code or go to: www.fabermusic.com/LangLangPianoMethodDownloads